FOREWORD

There are few moments over the course of a life that you can put your finger on and say "that is where my life changed". For me one of those moments was a meal. In 2007 I was working as a cook with little ambition in a vegetarian café when we booked for a family meal at Café Maitreya - Mark's previous restaurant. I was vaguely aware it had won some awards but nothing could have prepared me for what followed.

I had eaten at some high-end restaurants before, but my experience had always been forgettable. The food I ate that night was a revelation, the flavours were bold, clear and bright, the presentation was simple and beautiful and the technique was exact. I can still remember every course, every component. It was at that moment I decided I wanted to cook; I wanted to be a chef.

It is now eight years later and I own my own award-winning vegetarian restaurant in Bath but I am still striving to achieve the balance, skill and simplicity I tasted that night.

I have been fortunate enough to work with Mark on several occasions and I still haven't fathomed all the secrets of his food. When I heard that he was writing a book my first thought was "finally, finally I can learn how he does it". Every generation throws up a handful of chefs, whose cooking goes beyond just a meal. For me Mark is one of those chefs, and for vegetarians, Mark Evans and Tierra Kitchen should be the benchmark for simple food raised to the level of art.

Richard Buckley
Acorn Vegetarian Kitchen

CONTENTS

SOME STAPLES

SMALL DISHES

LUNCH BRUNCH DINNER

SWEET THINGS

At Tierra Kitchen our aim is simple: to make modern, vibrant, original dishes with a strong Mediterranean influence using the best local, seasonal and organic produce we can find, which is why we wanted to write a real cookbook with doable recipes using the same obtainable ingredients.

The recipes we have chosen include a selection of classic dishes that we developed firstly at Cafe Maitreya in Bristol and now at Tierra in Lyme Bay, like our tarte Tatin, samphire fritters and our super chocolate, plum and almond pudding, as well as those that customers frequently ask for like our tamari dip, carrot and almond cakes, and pickled blackcurrants.

But let's be honest, good vegetarian dishes take a touch more preparation than meat and two veg and a bit of effort is required for some of the recipes, so we've also included a section of staples and small dishes that are simpler with strong, clean flavours and textures.

Tierra Kitchen is a relaxed airy space with a stream-side terrace in the heart of Lyme Regis, but it's people who make a restaurant special and creative cooking possible, so big up to Katie, Cara and Natalie, and a special thank you to Head Chef Catalin Geanta who has contributed greatly to this book.

And of course, being able to produce these dishes relies on really good ingredients so we would like to give a loud cheer to John Roswell from Barrington for his excellent local vegetables, Ashley from Trill Farm for his superb organic salad and vegetables, Nick Stonex for her fantastic micro salad, A. David for their consistently good variety of produce, and James from RT Parris for the best local cheese and dairy produce.

We hope you enjoy trying these recipes at home, and we'd love to see how you get on so tweet us **@TierraKitchen** or get in touch via our Facebook page at **TierraKitchenLymeRegis.**

SOME STAPLES

TAMARI REDUCTION

This is really just a balsamic reduction with the addition of a quality soy sauce. However, the tamari gives the sauce a magic savoury dimension. We serve this as a dip with our homemade breads in the restaurant, but we also serve it with salads and use it as a seasoning to enrich the flavour of sauces.

400ml basic **balsamic vinegar**
400ml **red wine**
150g **caster sugar**
25ml **tamari**

Put all the ingredients in a medium-sized stainless steel pan and gently bring to the boil to ensure the sugar fully dissolves first. Reduce the liquid by just over 50 per cent or until the sauce coats the back of a wooden spoon. Cool and reserve for use.

This mix is great kept in a squeezy bottle for applying in moderate amounts.

TAMARI TOASTED PUMPKIN SEEDS

Tamari is a very fine, yet full-flavoured soy sauce from Japan. The pumpkin seeds are delicious and crispy after being dry-fried with the tamari and can be used in salads, pestos or simply eaten as a super tasty appetiser.

200g **pumpkin seeds**
4 dessert spoons **tamari**

Preheat the oven to 180°C.

Place the seeds in an ovenproof pan or thick tray and heat in the oven until hot through and just beginning to colour – approximately six to seven minutes.

Put the pan/tray onto a medium heated hob, pour the tamari evenly over the seeds and stir/dry-fry until the seeds are fully coated with the sauce and darkening.

Return the seeds to the oven for a further five minutes or until the seeds are dry and crisp. Stir again to ensure the seeds have not stuck, and allow to cool in the pan/tray.

TIERRA SIMPLE SPICE MIX

This spice combination can be used in humus and falafel mix, and is part of the base flavour for tagine. You will need a good spice/coffee blender.

2 dessert spoons **fennel seeds**
2 dessert spoons **coriander seeds**
2 dessert spoons **cumin seeds**

On a medium heat, gently toast the fennel seeds for a minute or so, or until just changing colour. Add the coriander and cumin seeds and toast for a further two minutes until they begin to brown and release their aromas. Allow to cool in the pan, then grind or blend to a fine powder.

LIGHT VEGETABLE STOCK

This versatile stock is used in many of our recipes. Unlike meat stocks, vegetable stocks are cooked quickly to capture the flavour of the vegetables' natural sugars, and become bitter and stewed if cooked too much.

MAKES 1.5 LITRES   **EQUIPMENT NEEDED:** 3 to 4 litre capacity stainless steel stock/saucepan

olive oil for cooking
3 medium **white onions**, peeled and rough chopped to 1cm cubes
5 cloves **garlic**, peeled and rough chopped
4 sticks **celery**, washed and sliced 1cm pieces
1 small to medium **leek**, washed and sliced into half cm pieces

4 medium **carrots**, peeled and cut into half cm pieces
2 **bay leaves**
1 good sprig **thyme**
10 **peppercorns**
1.8l **water**

Heat the stock pan on a medium heat, add the olive oil and the onions and sauté for four minutes until the onions start to become translucent. Add all the other ingredients, sauté and stir on a medium heat for five minutes, cooking without colour to release all the natural sugars in the vegetables.

Add the water, bring to the boil and simmer gently for 20 minutes. Strain, use immediately or cool and keep for up to three days in the fridge.

FINE POLENTA & CIDER BATTER

The cider gives the batter an incredible tangy flavour, the polenta a nuttiness. Vegan and gluten free.

200ml **cider**
70g **fine polenta/maize flour**
30g **cornflour**
good pinch of **sea salt flakes**

Mix the fine polenta and cornflour. Slowly add the cider whilst whisking to create a smooth batter. Season with fine sea salt flakes.

LEMON & THYME DRESSING

This light tangy dressing is particularly good with samphire, asparagus, fennel and avocado. This will keep comfortably for a few weeks in the fridge.

MAKES 300ML   **EQUIPMENT NEEDED:** good stand up/hand blender

3 medium sized **lemons**; 2 finely zested, all 3
  juiced
50ml **water**
3 dessert spoons **honey** or **maple syrup**
1 dessert spoon **Dijon mustard**

half a level teaspoon good **sea salt flakes**
4 sprigs **thyme**, leaves removed from the stalks
  and finely chopped
200ml **rapeseed oil**

Place the fine lemon zest, lemon juice and half the water in a small pan and gently bring to the boil. Reduce by half, to a thick pulp. NB: simmer gently to avoid the lemon mix colouring. Allow to cool in the pan for 10 minutes.

Transfer the lemon pulp to a blender/bowl, add the honey/maple syrup, the Dijon mustard, salt and chopped thyme. Blend for a minute until a smooth puree – there should be some small flecks of thyme remaining. Slowly add the rapeseed oil while blending (like a mayonnaise) to create a smooth emulsion. Finally blend in the remaining water; this will improve the consistency of the dressing and make it easier to pour.

PICKLED BLACKCURRANTS/BLACKBERRIES

This pickling recipe not only preserves these summer fruits, but helps give them a new aromatic dimension.

250g **blackcurrants or blackberries**
300g **water**
150g **cider vinegar**
150g **caster sugar**

3 **star anise**
3 **cloves**
2 **bay leaves**
2 sprigs **thyme**

Carefully pick out the connecting part of the stalk from the blackcurrants or carefully wash the blackberries. Place the fruit into sterilised Kilner or jam jars.

Place all the remaining ingredients in a pan and bring to the boil, stirring a little to ensure all the sugar dissolves.

Simmer for five minutes to infuse all the flavours.

Pour the hot liquid with all the seasoning gently over the fruit so it is totally covered and allow to cool.

NB: this recipe contains a fair bit of sugar, hence the pickled fruit can be served 24 hours later.

CHILLI & CRANBERRY RELISH

This super tangy relish is a great accompaniment to our chestnut falafel, pastries and savoury cheese dishes.

MAKES 500G

250g frozen **cranberries**
25ml **olive oil**
1 medium **red onion**, diced
2 cloves **garlic**, finely chopped
2 medium **red chillies**, seeded and
    finely chopped

1 medium **orange**, finely zested and juiced
half a **cinnamon stick**
1 **star anise**
50g **brown sugar**
25ml **raspberry vinegar**
50ml **cider vinegar**

Heat a small pan, add the olive oil, red onion, garlic and chilli, and sauté gently for three minutes. Add the cranberries, sugar, orange zest and juice, cinnamon and star anise, simmer and stir for three minutes more. Add the vinegars, stir well and simmer gently for 30 minutes. Stir a few times to ensure the relish is cooking evenly. Allow to cool in the pan.

ORANGE & ROSEMARY DRESSING

This versatile, tangy dressing will keep in the fridge for a good two weeks.

MAKES 200ML   **EQUIPMENT NEEDED:** blender

---

3 medium to large **oranges**, finely zested
   and juiced
1 teaspoon **English mustard**
1 heaped dessert spoon **honey**

half a teaspoon of fine **sea salt flakes**
2 sprigs **rosemary**, leaves finely chopped
2 large sprigs **thyme**
150ml **rapeseed oil**

Place the orange zest and juice in a small pan, gently bring to the boil and simmer until the liquid has reduced by half.

Allow the reduction to cool for five minutes, then transfer to a blender with the remaining ingredients except the rapeseed oil. Blend for 30 seconds until smooth, then add the oil slowly, little by little to make a smooth orange emulsion.

SICILIAN PARMESAN

This savoury seasoning was made at a time in Sicily when parmesan was unavailable or too expensive.

MAKES 300G   **EQUIPMENT NEEDED:** food processor

250g **old bread**, cut into rough chunks
4 cloves **garlic**, finely chopped
50g **parsley**, washed, shaken dry and roughly chopped
100ml **olive oil**

Place the bread, garlic and parsley into the food processor and blitz to a rough bread crumb mix.

Heat the olive oil in a good-sized pan on a moderate heat, add the bread crumb/garlic/parsley mix, and gently pan fry and stir until the crumbs are golden and the olive oil is absorbed. Allow to cool in the pan, then leave in a warm place so the mix becomes completely dry and crisp.

Keep in a sealed container in the store cupboard.

ORANGE BUTTERSCOTCH SAUCE

This is gluten- and dairy-free, and makes 250ml.

150g **golden syrup**
80g **caster sugar**
40g organic **dairy-free margarine**
1 medium **orange**, finely zested and juiced
150ml **soya cream**

Put all the ingredients, apart from the soya cream, into a good small saucepan, and gently bring to the boil, stirring a few times to ensure the sugar dissolves.

Simmer gently for six to eight minutes until the sauce becomes a rich golden colour and the boiling bubbles become smaller. NB: this sauce does not need to caramelise, as the orange will burn and become bitter.

Remove from the heat, allow to cool for a few minutes then whisk in the soya cream. This sauce can be served immediately or will keep for at least a month in the fridge.

DAIRY-FREE COCONUT ICE CREAM

This recipe makes one litre which is delicious as it is, but can be an excellent base for other flavour ice creams like chocolate or a variety of fruits; simply add the flavour/puree to the base before churning at a ratio of 80% base to 20% flavour/puree.

MAKES 1 LITRE   **EQUIPMENT NEEDED:** ice cream maker

800ml **coconut milk**
200ml **soya cream**
250g **caster sugar**
juice 1 **lemon**
optional: 1 **vanilla pod** (cut in half lengthways with the seeds scraped out)

Gently bring the coconut milk and soya cream to the boil (add the vanilla pods and seeds to infuse). Put the sugar into a good-sized bowl. Pour the hot coconut milk/soya onto the sugar and whisk to ensure the sugar dissolves. Allow the mixture to cool to room temperature, then add the lemon juice. The mixture is now ready to churn.

ALMOND BISCUITS

These nutty specials are vegan and gluten-free.

MAKES ABOUT 20 BISCUITS   **EQUIPMENT NEEDED:** food processor; two pieces of baking paper, 500mm long; a round biscuit cutter

250g **flaked almonds**, lightly toasted

50g **dairy-free margarine**

2 dessert spoons **maple syrup**

40g **caster sugar**

Preheat the oven to 160°C.

Blitz the almonds into rough breadcrumbs, add the margarine, maple syrup and caster sugar and blitz/pulse until the mix comes together as a paste. NB: the almonds should still retain some texture and not be powdered.

Transfer the mix into the centre of one piece of baking paper and form into a rectangle about 1cm thick. Place the second piece of baking paper on top and roll the mix out to a large rectangular shape, 2mm in thickness. Remove the top layer of baking paper and transfer the bottom paper and the rolled mix onto a baking tray. Cut the shapes of the biscuits using a cutter.

Bake at 160°C for 10 to 12 minutes, or until golden and firm. Allow to cool for 10 minutes until dry, then carefully remove the biscuit circles. Serve immediately or store in a tin for later. NB: these biscuits will keep nicely for a week.

ALMOND VANILLA CREAM

This delicious vegan, sugar-free cream takes two minutes to make and is a great alternative to dairy.

MAKES 450G   **EQUIPMENT NEEDED:** a good blender

225g whole blanched or flaked **almonds**

190g **almond milk**

2.5 dessert spoons **agave syrup**

1.5 dessert spoons **coconut oil**

seeds of one **vanilla pod** (cut in half lengthways; scrape out the seeds using the back of a small knife. Alternatively, use half teaspoon quality vanilla extract)

Simply blend all the ingredients together until smooth. Will keep for five days in the fridge.

SMALL DISHES

CARROT & ALMOND CAKES

with sesame, avocado and tamari reduction

These crispy little cakes are light and packed with flavour. We serve them as a starter in the restaurant but they also make a great canapé. Roasting the carrots first with rock salt seriously intensifies their flavour.

SERVES 6 **EQUIPMENT NEEDED:** 1m aluminium foil; food processor

6 medium **carrots**, (500g)
   washed and dried but not peeled
2 medium **shallots**, (100g) whole in skins
2 dessert spoons **rock salt**
6 cloves **garlic**
2 **star anise**
1 dessert spoon **fennel seeds**
1 teaspoon **black peppercorns**
4 **bay leaves**

320g ground **almond powder**
1 **lemon**, juiced
80g **sesame seeds**
salt and pepper for seasoning
25ml **olive oil**
30ml **tamari reduction**, *see recipe, page 10*
2 large ripe and ready to eat **avocados**
mixed salad leaves

Preheat the oven to 180°C.

Place the aluminium foil shiny side up in a small roasting pan, with most of the foil overlapping the sides. Sprinkle the rock salt evenly in the centre of the foil, sprinkle on the star anise, garlic, fennel seeds, peppercorns and bay leaves. Place the carrots and shallots evenly on top and fold in the sides of the foil to create an airtight parcel. Roast for 45 to 50 minutes, or until the carrots are cooked through.

Place the almond powder in a small roasting pan, and bake for 8 to 10 minutes, or until golden, and set aside to cool.

When the carrots are just cooked through, remove from the oven and allow to cool for 10 minutes or so, to enable them to be handled. Remove all traces of the seasoning from the carrots, garlic and shallots. Slice the carrots into 1cm pieces, remove the skin from the baked shallots and the garlic cloves, roughly chop and transfer all to a food processor, together with the lemon juice. Blitz for one minute until a rough puree, season with salt and pepper, transfer the mix to a bowl. Mix in the toasted almond powder to make a smooth pâté. Ideally allow the mix to stand in the fridge for at least half an hour before forming into cakes.

To serve: form the mix into small round cakes, approximately 3cm in diameter and 1cm thick. Dip the cakes into the sesame seeds to thoroughly coat each side. Pan fry the cakes lightly for one minute on each side in the olive oil until golden and crispy. Serve with the avocado, fresh salad leaves and one teaspoon of tamari reduction per serving.

CUCUMBER FRITTERS

with cider batter, pickled blackcurrants and Greek yoghurt

Simple, light and crispy with a delicate aromatic flavour, these gluten-free fritters are easy to make, and are vegan if you replace the Greek yoghurt.

SERVES 6   **EQUIPMENT NEEDED:** deep-fat fryer or good deep pan, plus 1.5 litres **rapeseed oil**

---

2 medium **cucumbers**
25ml good **cider vinegar**
1 teaspoon good **sea salt flakes**
300g fine **polenta and cider batter**, *see recipe, page 14*
200g pickled **blackcurrants**, *see recipe, page 16*
100g **Greek yoghurt**, optional

Peel the cucumbers, then cut sideways at a slight angle into 3mm thick pieces. Place in a bowl and sprinkle on the salt and vinegar, mix well and allow to marinate for twenty minutes.

To serve: heat the oil in the pan or deep fryer to 170°C. Dip six of the cucumber pieces into the batter and then into the hot oil. Fry for 30 seconds on each side until crisp and golden. Repeat with the remaining pieces. NB: as cucumbers have such a high water content, the fritters will initially be very hot, so allow them to cool a little.

Serve with fresh salad leaves and a couple of dessert spoons of pickled blackberries, plus a spoon of Greek yoghurt.

CHESTNUT FALAFELS

with chilli and cranberry relish

Falafels seem to be the new big fast food; protein packed, quick to serve, cheap and full of flavour and texture. We have tried to come up with a recipe bursting with crunch and nuts too, but it also works well with toasted pumpkin seeds substituted for the chestnuts.

SERVES 6   **EQUIPMENT NEEDED:** deep-fat fryer or good deep pan, plus 1 litre **rapeseed oil**

50ml **olive oil**

2 medium **shallots**, diced

4 cloves **garlic**, finely chopped

20g **Tierra spice mix**, *see recipe, page 12*

1 medium **red chilli**, seeded and finely chopped (optional)

200g cooked **chestnuts**

300g dried/500g cooked **chick peas**

1 **lemon**, finely zested and juiced

1 teaspoon good sea **salt flakes**

100g **gram (chick pea) flour**

For best results in making falafel it is best to soak and cook the chick peas; soak 300g of dried chick peas with 2 litres of water overnight. Thoroughly rinse the chick peas then place in a medium pan with 1.5 litres of cold water. Bring to the boil and simmer for 10 to 12 minutes until cooked through, then refresh under cold water until cooled. Make sure the chick peas are dry before using in the falafel mix. If using cooked tinned chick peas thoroughly rinse and then dry the peas. You may need to add a little extra gram flour to ensure the mix will fry properly.

Heat the olive oil in a small pan, add the diced shallots and sauté for three minutes until beginning to soften, then add the garlic, Tierra spice mix, plus the optional finely chopped chilli and sauté and stir for two minutes more.

Allow to cool in the pan for 10 minutes, then transfer to a food processor together with half the chick peas, lemon zest and juice, and the fine sea salt. Blitz/blend on high speed for two to three minutes until smooth. Transfer to a bowl.

Place the chestnuts in the food processor and blitz to a rough breadcrumb consistency – ie still a little chunky – then add to the smooth mix in the bowl. Place the remaining chick peas in the food processor and blitz to a similar rough consistency as the chestnuts, and add to the mix in the bowl. Finally, add the gram flour and mix thoroughly so all the elements are fully combined.

This mix is now ready to be cooked, or will keep in the fridge for four days.

To serve: roll the mix into small round falafels (half the size of a squash ball). Heat oil in a fryer or a deep pan to 170°C. Cook six at a time for two minutes until golden outside but thoroughly cooked through and crunchy in the centre.

Serve with chilli and cranberry relish (*see recipe, page 16*), fresh coriander, mint and/or natural yoghurt.

SWEET & SOUR RAINBOW PEPPERS

This multi-coloured, aromatic use of peppers is great to eat on its own as an appetiser or as part of a mezze. It can also be used as an accompaniment or added ingredient to tortillas, pasta, rice and cous cous. The original recipe was made with red pointed Romano peppers, which have a much better, sweeter flavour than the bell peppers. Simply use four of these instead, and cook for a few minutes less as they are slightly more delicate.

SERVES 6

50ml **olive oil**
1 **red onion**, peeled and cut downwards into
    quarters, separate the pieces (like petals)
3 **cloves**
2 cloves **garlic**, crushed
3 sprigs **thyme**, crushed

1 **red bell pepper**, 1 **green bell pepper**,
    1 **yellow bell pepper**, all deseeded and cut
    lengthways into strips 1.5cm thick
75g **sugar**
50ml **cider vinegar**
50ml **raspberry vinegar**
1 teaspoon good **sea salt flakes**

Place a good medium-sized pan on a moderate heat, add the olive oil, cloves and the red onion petals, gently sauté for three minutes until just beginning to soften, then add the garlic and thyme and sauté for two more minutes.

Add all the pepper strips, sea salt flakes and the sugar, gently sauté and stir for five minutes to ensure all the sugar is dissolved and the peppers are beginning to soften.

Finally, add the cider and raspberry vinegar, cook for a further 10 minutes, stirring regularly to ensure the peppers are cooked evenly in the liquor.

The dish is ready when the peppers are cooked through, but must still retain their texture. Allow to cool down completely in the pan to ensure maximum flavour absorption.

The sweet and sour peppers will keep in the fridge comfortably for at least a week.

BEETROOT CARPACCIO
red, orange and candy, with raspberry vinegar and horseradish crème fraiche

The description of this dish is a little misleading as a carpaccio is traditionally something that is served raw and finely sliced. However, by first roasting in a 'vacuum' with sea salt, herbs and spices, the beets gain a deep aromatic flavour which complement their natural earthiness, and still retain a great colour.

SERVES 6   **EQUIPMENT NEEDED:** 1m aluminium foil

---

3 large **beetroot**/6 medium beetroot (1.2 kilos in total), mixed colours are nice, cleaned with skins left on
4 dessert spoons **sea salt**
6 cloves **garlic**
4 **star anise**
4 **cloves**
1 dessert spoon **fennel seeds**
1 dessert spoon **coriander seeds**

2 sprigs **thyme**
50ml **raspberry vinegar**
3 dessert spoons **honey/maple syrup**
1 extra dessert spoon **sea salt flakes** to season the carpaccio
150g **crème fraiche**
40g **horseradish root**, finely grated with a little **lemon juice** to prevent discolouration

Preheat oven to 180°C.

Take the aluminium baking foil and place shiny side up in a small baking tray so the foil mainly overlaps the sides. Sprinkle four dessert spoons of the sea salt in the centre of the foil, then sprinkle on all of the spices and herbs, plus the garlic (except the horseradish root and the extra sea salt flakes, which are used later).

Place the beets on top of the salt and seasonings and fold in the sides of the aluminium foil to encase the beetroot in an airtight parcel. Place in the oven and bake for one and a half hours or until cooked through, but still firm. NB, if you are using smaller beets, cut down the cooking time accordingly. Allow to cool for at least 40 minutes.

Meanwhile, make the horseradish crème fraiche by thoroughly mixing the grated horseradish into the cream.

To serve, firstly remove the skin of the beets. Using a mandolin (or a very sharp knife) slice the beetroot into fine, 1mm thick pieces. Arrange on plates, displaying the different colours, or in a tray/container for later use (the carpaccio will keep for a week in the fridge). Splash the raspberry vinegar, the honey/maple syrup and the remaining sea salt evenly over the finely sliced beets. Serve with the horseradish crème fraiche.

TIERRA KITCHEN GAZPACHO

I was in two minds as to whether to include our gazpacho recipe or not due to the number of versions already available. However, it's here for the simple reason that our customers frequently ask about it. The lynch pin of a good gazpacho is the quality of the ingredients — particularly the tomatoes — and the roasted red peppers add a more velvety texture. This is best left to marinate for three hours before serving.

SERVES 6   **EQUIPMENT NEEDED:** blender

500g pointed **red peppers**, sliced in half lengthways, seeds and pith removed

25ml **extra virgin olive oil** to baste the peppers

50ml **extra virgin olive oil** to add to the gazpacho.

1kg best ripe **tomatoes**, washed and cut into eight pieces

4 medium **shallots** (250g), peeled and finely diced

6 large cloves **garlic**, peeled — 2 rough chopped to roast with the peppers, 4 finely chopped to marinate with the tomatoes

2 medium-sized **red chillies**, seeds removed and finely chopped

20g **mint leaves**, roughly chopped

20g **basil leaves**, roughly chopped

50ml **raspberry vinegar**

1 large **lemon**, juiced

1 dessert spoon **caster sugar**

1 teaspoon fine **sea salt**

to decorate...

100g **sugar snap peas**, sliced,

1 small **cucumber**, sliced,

Optional diced **peppers**, diced **red onion** and more fresh **mint** are all good

Preheat the oven to 180°C.

Baste the peppers with 25ml olive oil, 25ml raspberry vinegar, plus the two roughly chopped garlic cloves, season with one teaspoon of fine sea salt flakes and roast without colour for 30 to 40 minutes at 180°C, or until just cooked through. Allow to cool, then cut into four pieces ready to blend. Keep all the garlic and cooking juices to add to the gazpacho.

Mix all the other gazpacho ingredients together in a bowl. Allow to marinate for two hours at room temperature, then transfer to a blender together with the roast peppers and their cooking juices. Blend for two to three minutes, depending on how powerful the blender is, until the gazpacho is smooth. Transfer to the fridge and chill for at least one hour before serving.

Serve with the cucumber and sugar snaps. Gazpacho is also great with diced peppers, red onion, fresh mint and ice cubes.

SAMPHIRE FRITTERS

with lemon and thyme dressing

This dish was a real favourite at Cafe Maitreya in Bristol and continues to be at Tierra Kitchen. We use a mixture of locally foraged rock samphire and marsh samphire which comes from the east coast of the UK. Samphire is more readily available to buy these days in markets, farm shops, fish shops and even supermarkets. We also use a fine polenta and cider batter, which is vegan and gluten free. In the restaurant we serve the fritters with fine marinated fennel: very finely shaved fennel marinated with lemon, honey and fine sea salt.

SERVES 4 / 12 FRITTERS   **EQUIPMENT NEEDED:** deep-fat fryer or a good-sized deep pan for
                                                                                     deep frying

---

250g **samphire**, washed, shaken dry, with the hard part of the stem removed

300g fine **polenta and cider batter**, *see recipe, page 14*

1.5 litres **rapeseed oil**

100ml **lemon and thyme dressing**, *see recipe, page 14*

Prepare a tray with sheets of kitchen towel on top, ready to absorb any excess oil from the cooked fritters.

Heat up the rapeseed oil in the fryer/pan to 170°C.

Pour the polenta and cider batter into a good-sized bowl and give it a quick whisk so it is a smooth, thick consistency.

Take four tennis ball sized clusters of samphire, dip and coat in the batter, then carefully drop the balls into the fryer. The samphire will soufflé a little and expand to irregular shapes but don't worry; the fritters will look a bit like crazy birds' nests. Fry for two minutes until the fritters are golden and crisp, then transfer the fritters onto the kitchen towel. Repeat two more times until all the samphire is used.

Serve the fritters immediately, drizzled with the lemon and thyme dressing.

GREEN HUMUS

The addition of fresh coriander and parsley gives our humus a wonderful aromatic depth of flavour, as well as a striking colour. We do not use any tahini in this recipe, as we've found the sweetness does not quite work with the aromatic herbs. Using cannellini beans instead of chick peas also works very well, with an even deeper green colour.

MAKES 700G   **EQUIPMENT NEEDED:** food processor/blender

70ml **olive oil**

2 **medium shallots**, diced

2 **cloves garlic**, finely chopped

25g **Tierra spice mix**, *see recipe, page 12*

500g cooked **chick peas**, thoroughly rinsed and
   then dried

1 **lemon**, finely zested and juiced

juice of 1 **orange**

50g **parsley**, chopped

50g **coriander**, chopped

1 teaspoon good **sea salt flakes**

Put a pan on a medium heat, add the olive oil and diced shallots, sauté for two to three minutes until becoming translucent, add the finely chopped garlic and Tierra spice mix, sauté for three more minutes. Allow to cool.

Add all the contents of the pan, plus all the other ingredients to a food processor/blender. Blend or puree on a high speed for three minutes, or until the humus is completely smooth and green. NB: you may need to add a little water to ensure the smoothness of the humus.

This will keep in the refrigerator for four days.

PISTACHIO CHORIZO

This deep-flavoured savoury treat can be served as an accompaniment with a host of dishes like paella and tagine, or just as a pâté with pitta and olives. It's delicious in a sandwich with avocado and sorrel leaves.

SERVES 12

EQUIPMENT NEEDED: narrow terrine mould or something similar to mirror a traditional chorizo shape; food processor

50ml **olive oil**
250g **pistachios**, shelled
1 teaspoon fine **sea salt**
2 level teaspoons **smoked paprika**
1 medium **onion**, finely diced
4 cloves **garlic**, finely chopped
2 medium **red chillies**, deseeded and
    finely chopped

80ml **red wine**
200ml **tomato passata**
2 level teaspoons **agar agar powder**
50g **butter**, melted
120g **mature cheddar**, finely grated

Preheat the oven to 180°C.

Baste the pistachios with half the olive oil, one teaspoon of smoked paprika, plus half the fine sea salt. Roast in the oven for four minutes until crispy and just taking colour, then set aside to cool.

Place a small to medium pan on a moderate heat, add the olive oil and diced onion and sauté for three minutes. Add the garlic, finely chopped chilli and the remaining teaspoon of smoked paprika, and sauté gently for two minutes more. Add the red wine, gently simmer for two minutes, then add the tomato passata and bring back to the boil. Add the agar agar flakes, gently simmer and stir for three minutes to ensure the flakes fully dissolve. Transfer to a good-sized bowl.

Blitz the pistachios in a food processor to a rough breadcrumb consistency, then mix the pistachios into the tomato/red wine base. Finally, mix in the melted butter, grated cheese, and the remaining sea salt. Mix thoroughly until fully incorporated and smooth.

Line the chosen mould with cling film to ensure easy removal once the chorizo has set. Transfer the chorizo mix equally into the mould, using a palette knife to pack it down. Allow to cool for 30 minutes, then encase fully in the cling film and chill for at least one hour to set.

The chorizo will keep for 10 days in the fridge.

SUMAC & ALMOND PESTO

The sweetness of the almonds and raisins together with the lemony sumac are particularly delicious with asparagus. In the summer we also serve this pesto with pan-fried samphire and locally foraged Lyme Bay sea kale. A little tossed in a pan with some curly kale or chard can also be a winter flavour treat, as well as adding a funky purple colour.

MAKES ABOUT 400G **EQUIPMENT NEEDED:** food processor

25ml **olive oil**, for cooking
1 small to medium **red onion**, peeled and
    finely diced
1 large clove **garlic**, peeled and finely chopped
80g good **raisins**

2 dessert spoons **sumac**
80g **flaked almonds**, lightly toasted
1 **lemon**, juiced
120ml **olive oil**, to add to the pesto
1 teaspoon fine **sea salt**

Place a small pan on a medium heat, add 25ml olive oil and the diced red onion, sauté and stir for three minutes until the onion is just softening. Add the garlic and the sumac, gently sauté and stir for two minutes more, then add the raisins, sauté and stir for a further four minutes on a gentle heat so the raisins are softening. Remove the mix from the heat and allow to cool in the pan for 15 minutes.

Transfer the mix to a food processor together with the toasted almonds, lemon juice, salt and 120ml olive oil. Blitz/blend until a grainy purple pesto. This pesto is better with a little bite; if it becomes too smooth the raisins will make it set and the pesto will then have a slightly odd texture.

TO SERVE WITH ASPARAGUS

400g asparagus makes a handsome starter or a side dish for four.

Trim and blanch the asparagus with lemony, salted water until al dente. Refresh the asparagus in cold water.

Place a good-sized sauté pan or wok on a medium heat, add 40ml olive oil, plus 80g of the sumac almond pesto. Stir the pesto into the olive oil to break it down a little, then add the blanched asparagus, sauté and stir for two minutes until the asparagus has a coating of pesto and is just beginning to take colour. Serve immediately.

LUNCH BRUNCH DINNER

APPLEWOOD CHEDDAR TARTE TATIN

with roast butternut squash, caramelised red onion, sun blushed tomato and pine nut dressing

This delicious all-butter puff pastry upside down bake takes a little preparation but has a real wow factor on presentation. The roast squash, caramelised red onion and slightly sweet smoked cheddar work together perfectly, while the dressing adds extra tang and colour. Great served with something fresh and green like sautéed pak choi or cavolo nero.

SERVES 4 **EQUIPMENT NEEDED:** a 20cm flan mould or shallow dish, with a depth of 1.5 to 2cm; baking paper to fit and overlap the mould/dish

---

TO MAKE THE TARTE TATIN

800g **butternut squash**, peeled, seeds removed and cut into 1cm cubes (prepared weight should be close to 600g)

50ml **olive oil**

1 dessert spoon **honey**

1 level teaspoon fine **sea salt flakes**

2 medium **red onions** (approximately 300g) peeled and finely sliced

30g **pumpkin seeds**

230g **smoked Applewood cheddar**

250g all-butter **puff pastry**

Preheat the oven to 180°C.

Baste the butternut squash cubes with half of the olive oil and the honey on a non-stick baking tray and season with the sea salt. Roast for 25 to 30 minutes until just cooked through and taking colour.

Meanwhile, in a small pan sauté the sliced red onion with the remaining olive oil on a gentle heat for about ten minutes until it's just beginning to caramelise and turn a rich burgundy colour. Allow to cool for 10 minutes in the pan, then transfer into a sieve and leave to drain for a further 10 minutes. Collect the excess drained oil to add to the sun blushed tomato dressing.

Grease and line the baking dish/flan mould with baking parchment so the parchment overlaps the dish by 3cm. Evenly scatter on the pumpkin seeds. Cut the Applewood cheddar into thin slices, 2.5mm thick, and evenly cover the bottom of the dish over the pumpkin seeds.

On a flat, lightly floured surface, carefully roll out the puff pastry to the shape of the dish/mould and allow 2cm overlap all around. The pastry should be 3mm thick. Let the pastry rest for five minutes and reset the oven temperature to 200°C.

continued...

Now finish assembling the Tatin: evenly layer the roast butternut squash on top of the Applewood cheddar, then evenly spread on the caramelised red onion. Finally, place the pastry on top so that all the filling is enveloped with 2cm of pastry overlapping all around the tart.

Bake at 200°C for 20 to 25 minutes or until the pastry has risen, is crisp and golden brown.

Allow the tart to rest for two minutes. For an excellent finish, place the bottom of the tart on a gentle to medium heat for a minute or two to caramelise and colour the cheese at the base.

Turn the tart out to expose the cheese, either onto a chopping board or serving plate. Portion with a sharp knife, serve with the dressing and optional extra greens.

TO MAKE THE DRESSING

150g **sun blushed tomatoes**, drained and chopped into small pieces
40g **pine nuts**, toasted
1 clove **garlic**, very finely chopped
25ml **cider vinegar**
40ml **olive oil**, plus any excess juice from the cooked **red onion**
1 dessert spoon **honey**

To make the sun blushed tomato and pine nut dressing mix all the ingredients together and ideally allow to stand and marinate for one hour.

ROMANO PEPPER ROULADE
WITH CARROT & CASHEW FILLING

spring greens and plum tomato and caper dressing

This visually stunning roulade is great served hot or cold. Romano peppers are in a different flavour league to the Dutch bell peppers which are forced all year round. The best time to make this dish is in spring or early summer with Spanish peppers, English spring carrots and greens. NB: this dish is best prepared in advance, allowing it to set a little in the fridge before slicing and reheating.

SERVES 6

EQUIPMENT NEEDED: food processor; 1 piece aluminium foil, 1m in length; 2 pieces of baking paper, 500mm in length

---

TO MAKE THE ROULADE

1 bunch **spring carrots**, 500g, greens removed, washed and shaken dry

2 medium **shallots**, 150g, kept whole in skins

Seasoning to roast the carrots: 4 dessert spoons **rock salt**, 4 **star anise**, 6 **cloves**, 6 cloves **garlic**, 1 dessert spoon **black peppercorns**, 1 dessert spoon **fennel seeds**, 1 dessert spoon **coriander seeds**

9 to 10 large **Romano/pointed red peppers**, 900g to 1kg

100ml **olive oil**

25ml **raspberry vinegar**

1 teaspoon fine **sea salt flakes** to season the peppers

450g **cashew nuts**

1 **lemon**, juiced

2 teaspoons fine **sea salt flakes** to season the spring greens

300g **spring greens**, washed with the tough stem removed from each leaf

Preheat the oven to 180°C.

Firstly roast the carrots: line a small baking tray with aluminium baking foil so the foil overlaps the sides. Sprinkle the rock salt evenly on the foil, then evenly sprinkle the remaining seasoning ingredients onto the salt. Place the carrots on top together with the two whole shallots and six garlic cloves, fold the foil inwards to encase the carrots into a parcel. This cooking method ensures the carrots cook in an airtight parcel and absorb more of the flavour from the seasoning. Bake the carrots for 35 to 45 minutes or until just cooked through.

Meanwhile, slice the peppers in half lengthways and remove all the seeds. Baste the peppers in half the olive oil and the raspberry vinegar, season with sea salt and place on a baking tray. Roast the peppers for 30 to 40 minutes without colouring so they are just cooked through. Allow to cool.

continued...

In a good-sized frying pan or wok, gently sauté the spring greens with a sprinkle of sea salt flakes in the remaining olive oil (in a few batches) to soften and slightly wilt them. Place to one side and allow to cool, ready to assemble the roulade.

Place the cashew nuts on a baking tray and bake for 5 minutes at 170°C or until just beginning to take colour. Allow to cool for five minutes, then blitz in a food processor until a rough breadcrumb consistency. Place the powdered cashews in a mixing bowl.

When the carrots are cooked, remove from the foil and the seasoning together with the shallots and garlic cloves, roughly chop while still hot and transfer to a food processor with the lemon juice. Remove the skins from the shallots and the garlic cloves, roughly chop and add to the chopped carrots. Blitz for one minute until the mix is a grainy puree, transfer to a bowl and mix in the cashew powder to make a moist pâté. Season with a teaspoon of fine sea salt and allow to cool for 20 minutes.

To assemble the roulade: place the baking paper on a flat surface. Place the peppers side by side to form a rectangle in the centre of the paper. Evenly cover the peppers with the Spring Greens to form a green layer. Place the carrot/cashew pâté in a sausage shape in the centre of the rectangle. Using the paper as leverage, roll the roulade so the pâté is firmly enveloped in the centre. Use the paper as a holding device around the roulade to keep its shape round. Place the roulade in the centre of the second piece of baking paper and roll again.

Place in the fridge for at least one hour. The roulade can now be portioned: using a very sharp knife, slice through the paper into six portions. Either serve cold or reheat at 180°C for 10 minutes and serve. NB: if serving hot, place the portions into the oven with the baking paper still around the roulades to help maintain their shape.

TO MAKE THE DRESSING

50ml **olive oil**
2 medium **shallots**, finely diced
2 large cloves **garlic**, finely chopped
200g **cherry plum tomatoes**, washed and cut
    in halves

50g **caster sugar**
50ml **cider vinegar**
sprig of **thyme**
50g **baby capers**, or chopped **normal capers**,
    rinsed and shaken dry

Place a small pan on a medium heat, add the olive oil and the diced shallots, sauté and stir for three minutes. Add the garlic, sauté and stir for two minutes more. Add the cherry plum tomato halves, the sugar, salt, thyme and the vinegar, cook gently for eight minutes or until the tomatoes are just cooked, but still retain their shape and texture. Mix in the mini capers/pieces while the sauce is hot and allow to cool completely in the pan for maximum flavour absorption.

PUMPKIN SEED, SAGE & CHEDDAR SAUSAGES

with mustard, yoghurt mayonnaise

We love these sausages at Tierra Kitchen. They now seem to be a permanent fixture on our brunch and children's menus. A combination of roasting the butternut squash and toasting the pumpkin seeds in soy sauce gives the sausage mix a great depth of flavour. The sausages can easily be vegan: simply leave out the cheddar and serve with a different sauce.

MAKES 10 FAT SAUSAGES   **EQUIPMENT NEEDED:** food processor

800g **butternut squash**, peeled, seeds removed and cut into 1cm cubes (prepared weight should be close to 650g)

20ml **olive oil**, 1 level teaspoon fine **sea salt flakes** to roast the squash with

20ml **olive oil** for frying the onion

1 medium to large **onion** (200g), peeled and finely diced

2 large cloves **garlic**, finely chopped

200g **pumpkin seeds**, blitzed in a food processor to a breadcrumb consistency

12 **sage leaves**, finely chopped

220g fine **breadcrumbs** (preferably panko, as lighter and more refined)

120g good **mature cheddar cheese**, grated

2 dessert spoons **tamari** (or a similar light soy sauce)

1 teaspoon good fine **sea salt**

50ml plus of **olive oil** for frying the sausages once prepared

80g **mayonnaise**

80g **natural yoghurt**

40g **grain mustard**

1 clove **garlic**, very finely grated

Preheat the oven to 180°C.

Place the prepared squash in a baking dish, baste with the olive oil and sea salt. Roast in a preheated oven for 30 to 40 minutes until just cooked through and taking colour. Allow to cool for 10 minutes.

Now fry the onion in 20ml of olive oil on a gentle heat for three minutes, add the garlic and fry for a further two minutes until the onion becomes translucent. Remove from the heat and allow to cool for 10 minutes.

Finally, in a large bowl, mix together the squash, pumpkin seed crumbs, cooked onion and garlic with the chopped sage, breadcrumbs, cheddar, tamari and fine sea salt. Break up the squash by hand and pinch it into the other ingredients to form the sausage mix. The squash should still retain some texture and be recognisable. It is best to chill the mixture for at least 30 minutes before rolling. The mix will keep for five days in the fridge.

continued...

Allow the mix to stand in the fridge before rolling and pan frying. To roll, take small tennis ball-sized amounts of the mix, roll into a firm ball first before rolling into fat sausages on a clean surface. To cook, pan fry gently for about four minutes. NB: these sausages need a gentle heat and constant turning as they take colour very easily.

To make the mustard and yoghurt sauce, simply mix together the mayonnaise, yoghurt, grain mustard and the garlic.

CROWN PRINCE PUMPKIN & SAGE GRATINÉE

with hazelnut crust, sautéed chestnut mushrooms and hazelnut sauce

The smell of this delicious squash cooking with sage, ginger and coconut always lifts the spirits on a cold November day. A vegan and gluten-free dish, the combination of the buttery squash and sage, sautéed mushrooms and creamy hazelnut sauce ticks all the boxes for autumn flavour and texture.

SERVES 6　　　　　　　　**EQUIPMENT NEEDED:** food processor with a slicer/mandolin; 25cm x 25cm baking dish with a 6cm depth

---

TO MAKE THE GRATIN

1.5kg **Crown Prince pumpkin**

600g **jacket potatoes**, peeled

4 large cloves **garlic**, peeled and finely chopped

2cm fresh **ginger root**, peeled and finely chopped

3 medium **shallots**, peeled and finely sliced

2 medium **chillies**, seeded and finely chopped

15 **sage leaves**, finely chopped

1 dessert spoon **Dijon mustard**

500ml **coconut milk**

1 dessert spoon chopped **fresh thyme**

1 teaspoon fine **sea salt flakes**

quarter of a teaspoon **ground black pepper**

250g whole skinless **roasted hazelnuts** (for the topping)

40ml **olive oil** (for the topping)

Preheat the oven to 160°C.

Carefully cut the Crown Prince into eight segments with a large sharp knife. Remove the hard outer skin and the seeds and pith, slice to a thickness of 1mm and place the slices in a large bowl. Peel the potatoes, slice to the same thickness as the pumpkin and add to the bowl. Add all the remaining gratin ingredients (except the hazelnuts and olive oil), and mix in thoroughly by hand. It is important to break up the slices of squash and potato really well to ensure all are thoroughly coated in all the seasoning and coconut milk and cook evenly.

Transfer the mix to the gratin dish/deep tray, pressing the slices down evenly and into the corners with all the seasoning. Cover the top with baking parchment to prevent the gratin from taking too much colour during cooking. Bake at 160°C for one hour and fifteen minutes or until a knife just penetrates the gratin.

To make the hazelnut crust: blitz the hazelnuts very quickly so they are just a bit crushed, like rough breadcrumbs with chunks. Mix in the olive oil and season well with sea salt and pepper. Remove the baking parchment from the top of the gratin and evenly distribute the blitzed hazelnuts on top. Place back in the oven for a further 10 minutes at 180°C to colour and lightly crisp the topping.

continued...

TO MAKE THE HAZELNUT SAUCE

25ml **olive oil**

2 medium **shallots**, peeled and finely sliced

2 large cloves **garlic**, peeled and finely chopped

1 level dessert **Dijon mustard**

2 dessert spoons **tamari**

250ml **coconut milk**

200ml light **vegetable stock**

half a teaspoon **fine sea salt**

200g whole skinless **roasted hazelnuts**

250g **chestnut mushrooms** cut into 4mm slices,

50ml **olive oil** and fine **sea salt flakes**

   for cooking

Place a small saucepan on a medium heat, add the olive oil and sliced shallots, sauté for three minutes until the shallots are becoming translucent, then add the garlic and sauté for two minutes more. Add the mustard and tamari, stir in well. Add the stock and coconut milk and bring to the boil, and simmer for five minutes to infuse all the flavours together. Transfer to a blender/food processor together with the hazelnuts and blend for two to three minutes until the sauce is a rich, smooth consistency similar to double cream.

Finally, sauté the mushrooms: place a large sauté pan/wok on a medium to high heat, add 25ml olive oil plus half the mushroom chunks and sauté for two minutes until golden and crisp, and season well. Repeat with the second half of the mushrooms. Serve immediately with the hazelnut sauce and the gratin.

CAERPHILLY CHEESE & ALMOND SOUFFLÉ

with roast parsnips, orange and rosemary dressing

Caerphilly cheese reminds me of feta with its crumbly texture and slight salty tinge. It has a mellow nutty flavour, with a zesty freshness which beautifully matches almonds. Caerphilly varies greatly in quality so it is worth spending a little more for this special occasion recipe. It seems a lot of Caerphilly contains animal rennet, so be sure to check. This can be a 'twice baked' recipe, allowing you to bake the first time in advance, and pop the soufflé back in the oven when required.

SERVES 6

EQUIPMENT NEEDED: baking dish 20cm x 20cm, with a depth of 4cm; oven dish large enough to accommodate the baking dish plus enough water for a 2cm depth; good roasting tray for the parsnips. A mixer makes preparation a lot quicker

---

400ml **milk**

1 small **onion**, peeled and roughly chopped

2 **cloves**

a good pinch **nutmeg**

1 **bay leaf**

1 sprig **thyme**

50g **butter**

100g **self-raising flour**

180g **Caerphilly cheese**

5 **egg yolks**

8 **egg whites**

50g **flaked almonds**, toasted

10 to 12 small **parsnips**, 800g

2 **oranges**, finely zested

30ml **olive oil** for basting

1 level teaspoon fine **sea salt flakes** and a good
   twist of **milled pepper** to season

120ml **orange and rosemary dressing**,
   see recipe, page 18

Preheat the oven to 180°C.

Firstly prepare the parsnips: peel and place whole in a pan with enough cold water to cover, season with salt and bring to the boil. Simmer for three minutes, remove from the heat and transfer the parsnips onto a tray to cool down. Set aside while making the soufflé.

To make the soufflé, place the milk, onion, cloves, nutmeg, bay and thyme in a small pan and slowly bring to the boil. Simmer gently for three minutes to infuse the flavours into the milk. Meanwhile, in a small thick-bottomed pan, melt the butter and mix in the self-raising flour to form a roux. Strain the infused milk and whisk into the roux on a gentle heat, slowly at first, to produce a thick smooth white 'base' (very thick sauce).

continued...

Allow the base sauce to cool for five minutes, then transfer to a bowl/mixer. Beat in the egg yolks, then immediately beat in the Caerphilly cheese until the mix is smooth and the cheese is fully incorporated.

Allow to cool for 10 minutes and, meanwhile, whisk the egg whites until peaking and stiff.

When the cheese sauce mix is almost down to room temperature, carefully fold in the egg whites in two lots to ensure the mix is light and airy. Finally, mix in the toasted almonds and season with fine sea salt flakes.

Transfer the mix into the baking dish, place in the oven tray with enough water to surround the soufflé with a 2cm depth. NB: alternatively, this mix will make 6 to 8 individual soufflés in 6oz ramekins.

Bake for 20 minutes at 180°C or until the soufflé has doubled in size and is firm to the touch in the centre. Simultaneously roast the prepared parsnips: baste the cooked parsnips with the olive oil, orange zest and fine sea salt, roast for 20 minutes until golden and crisp. Serve the parsnips with the soufflé and some orange rosemary dressing.

EARLY SUMMER WARM SALAD

with samphire, peas, pistachio and toasted halloumi, and rhubarb anise dressing

The combination of fresh samphire, crispy early summer new potatoes with tender new season spinach and peas with a tangy rhubarb dressing is a real favourite at Tierra. The dish is gluten-free, and can be vegan by leaving out the halloumi.

SERVES 4

EQUIPMENT NEEDED: large sauté pan/wok; blender to make the rhubarb dressing

25ml **olive oil**

300g small **new potatoes**, precooked in their skins, then cut in halves

3 **Romano/pointed red peppers**, 300g, sliced in half lengthways, then cut into quarters with the seeds removed

1 level teaspoon fine **sea salt flakes**

160g **samphire**, with the sinewy part of the stem removed, washed and shaken dry

4 **spring onions**, washed and cut

20g **fresh dill** or 2 sprigs **thyme**, stems removed

100g **spinach**, washed and shaken dry with the stalks removed

200g **peas in pods**, pods removed

50g **pistachios**, lightly toasted

250g **halloumi**, sliced sideways into 8 pieces

80g **mixed small salad leaves** like rocket, watercress, baby spinach

For the rhubarb anise dressing

200g **rhubarb**, washed and sliced into 1cm chunks

50ml **water**

1 dessert spoon **caster sugar**

2 **star anise**

Firstly make the rhubarb dressing: place the rhubarb, 50ml water, caster sugar and star anise in a small pan and bring to the boil slowly on a low heat. Simmer for 10 minutes until all the rhubarb is soft. Allow to cool completely in the pan, then remove the star anise and blend until a smooth puree.

To make the warm salad: place a large sauté pan on a gentle heat and add the olive oil with the sliced potatoes and the red pepper pieces. Sauté very gently for five minutes so the peppers are beginning to soften and the potatoes are colouring and beginning to crisp, and season with the fine sea salt. Turn up the heat a bit and add the samphire, spring onion pieces plus the dill or thyme, stir fry for two minutes then add the spinach and the peas, stir fry for a further two minutes until the spinach has wilted and the peas are just beginning to soften, and then remove from the heat.

Meanwhile, either toast the halloumi under a grill or sauté until golden brown in a hot pan with a little olive oil. This should only take a few minutes.

continued...

To serve the salad: plate the crispy potatoes, then layer on the samphire with the peas, spring onion, spinach and pepper. Add some fresh leaves and sprinkle on some pistachio. Finally, add two pieces of toasted halloumi per person and two dessert spoons of rhubarb dressing.

FIVE WINTER VEGETABLE TAGINE

with figs, raz al hanout, giant cous cous and toasted almonds

A real favourite at Tierra Kitchen, we have tried to recreate this Moroccan classic as simply as possible while retaining a sweet, floral depth of flavour. The dish can be prepared and served immediately, but preparing it a day in advance and allowing the tagine to cool completely in the pan seriously adds to the flavour.

SERVES 6　　　　　　**EQUIPMENT NEEDED:**　good-sized tagine or saucepan

---

TO MAKE THE TAGINE

- 50ml **extra virgin olive oil**
- 2 medium **onions**, peeled and diced
- 4 large cloves **garlic**, peeled and finely chopped
- 2 medium **red chillies**, seeds removed and finely chopped
- 40g **Tierra spice mix**, *see recipe, page 12*
- 1 heaped dessert spoon quality **tomato puree**
- 1 large / 2 small **preserved lemons**, finely diced
- 2 sprigs **thyme**
- 1 small **butternut squash**, 600g, peeled, seeds removed and cut into 1.5cm cubes
- 1 medium **leek**, washed and sliced into 1cm rounds

- 3 large **carrots**, approx. 300g, peeled and cut into 1.5cm chunks
- half a **celeriac**, approx. 500g, peeled and cut into 1.5cm cubes
- 2 medium **parsnips**, approx. 400g, peeled and cut into 1.5cm chunks
- 600ml **vegetable stock**
- 180g dried, ready-to-eat **figs**
- good-sized pinch of quality **saffron**
- 1 teaspoon fine **sea salt flakes** and freshly ground **black pepper** to taste
- 50g **flaked almonds**, toasted
- 80g **yoghurt** (optional) to serve

Place the tagine/saucepan on a medium heat, add the olive oil and the diced onion, sauté and stir for three minutes. Add the garlic and chilli, sauté and stir for two more minutes, then add the spice mix, tomato paste, thyme and preserved lemon, stir well and sauté for one more minute. Add the remaining olive oil, then all the butternut squash, the leek and carrot chunks, stir well to coat the vegetables with the olive oil and seasoning, sauté and stir for five minutes. Add the celeriac cubes, sauté and stir for five minutes more, then add the stock. Bring to the boil, then reduce the heat to a slow simmer to ensure the vegetables cook slowly with all the seasoning, add the parsnips and simmer for 30 minutes.

Finally add the figs, the saffron, and one teaspoon fine sea salt, simmer for a further five minutes to fully infuse all the flavours. Allow the tagine to stand in the pan for as long as possible before serving, for maximum flavour absorption.

continued...

TO MAKE THE GIANT COUS COUS

700ml **light vegetable stock**, *see recipe, page 12*

400g **giant cous cous**

80ml **olive oil**

1.5 teaspoons fine **sea salt flakes**

1 medium **red onion**, peeled and finely diced

2 large cloves **garlic**, peeled and very finely chopped

1 **green pepper**, seeds removed and cut into 1cm cubes

Bring 400ml of the stock to the boil in a medium saucepan together with 40ml of olive oil and one teaspoon of fine sea salt. Add the cous cous and turn the heat down low to a simmer, cook gently for eight minutes, adding the remaining stock intermittently, a little like making a risotto. Remove from the heat, break up the cous cous a little with a wooden spoon and allow to cool for 10 to 15 minutes.

Meanwhile, place a good-sized saucepan/wok on a medium heat, add the remaining olive oil and the diced red onion, sauté and stir for three minutes then add the finely chopped garlic and sauté for two minutes more. Add the green pepper, sauté and stir for five minutes to soften the peppers.

Transfer the cous cous to a large bowl, break it using a wooden spoon to prevent lumps. Add the red onion and green pepper, season with the remaining fine sea salt flakes.

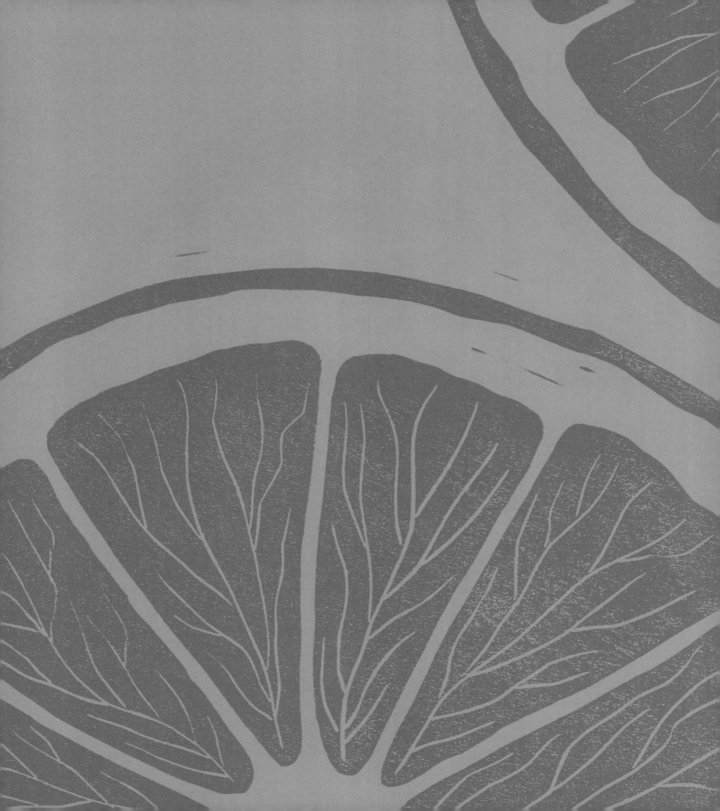

SWEET THINGS

CHOCOLATE & PASSION FRUIT DÉLICE

with passion fruit puree and almond cream

The combination of rich chocolate ganache and piquant passion fruit works all year round. This layered tart is vegan, gluten-free and sugar-free.

MAKES 8 PORTIONS   **EQUIPMENT NEEDED:** 20cm loose-bottomed flan case with a 1 inch depth; food processor; greaseproof paper

---

15 fresh **passion fruit**
120ml **water**
3 dessert spoons **agave syrup** /
   60g **caster sugar**
200g **gluten-free digestive biscuits** /
   200g **ordinary digestives**

100g **dairy-free margarine**
500ml **soya cream**
100g **glucose syrup**
300g **dark chocolate pistoles** / small pieces
   with 70% cocoa solids
1.5 level teaspoons **agar agar powder**

Firstly make the passion fruit puree: cut the passion fruit in half and scoop out all the fruit and seeds into a small saucepan. Add the water and the agave syrup/sugar and gently bring to the boil. Simmer and stir for five minutes to loosen all the sticky pulp from the seeds. Using a spatula, pass the passion fruit pulp through a conical strainer/sieve. NB: you will have to press hard to free all the puree from the fruit. Set the puree aside to cool.

Grease the flan case, then line tightly with the greaseproof paper and trim the paper around the top.

To make the base: blitz the digestives in a food processor to a rough breadcrumb consistency. Thoroughly mix 40g of the dairy-free margarine into the biscuit crumb mix. Evenly press into the bottom of the lined flan case to form a firm biscuit base.

To make the chocolate ganache: measure 400ml of the soya cream into a small saucepan, add the glucose syrup and gently bring to the boil, simmer on a gentle heat for one minute to ensure the glucose syrup dissolves properly. Remove from the heat and allow to cool for ten minutes, to about 50°C. Transfer to a bowl and beat in the chocolate with a whisk/wooden spoon until melted, fully incorporated and smooth. Beat in the remaining 60g dairy-free margarine until smooth and glossy. In a separate bowl gently whisk the remaining soya cream until it doubles (soya cream will not peak in the same way dairy cream will). Fold the beaten soya into the chocolate mix, pour evenly onto the biscuit base and place in the fridge to set for at least an hour.

continued...

Finally complete the passion fruit layer and sauce: measure 200ml of the passion fruit puree (keep the remainder as a sauce to serve with the delice), put in a small pan and bring to the boil. Whisk in 1.5 level teaspoons of agar agar powder, simmer and whisk for two minutes. Remove from heat and allow to cool for 10 minutes. It is best to test that the passion fruit will set properly by putting a teaspoon of it onto a cold plate and popping in the fridge for five minutes. If the passion fruit has not set, return to the boil with a further half a teaspoon of agar agar and simmer for two minutes more. Once you are sure the puree is ready, evenly pour onto the chocolate layer of the delice. Allow to cool and set by placing back in the fridge for at least an hour.

To serve: slice into eight portions with a sharp knife, serve with the remaining passion fruit puree, and a dollop of almond cream, *see recipe, page 22.*

ROSEHIP POACHED PEARS

with Turkish delight

I have been in two minds as whether or not to include this recipe. On one hand rosehips are difficult when processing into syrup at home, the syrup is a little difficult to get hold of in the shops, plus due to added sugar content, the flavour of the product is subtle. On the other hand, rosehips are an important part of culinary history in Europe, have a subtle but definite flavour and grow wild practically all over the UK.

SERVES 6

EQUIPMENT NEEDED: 1 piece greaseproof paper, cut to the size of the poaching pan; 20cm x 20cm tray with a depth of 2.5cm, or similar vessel to set the Turkish delight in

TO MAKE THE PEARS

6 **red plums**, 1 dessert spoon **sugar**, 50ml **water**; to make a plum puree
6 **portion-sized pears**, ideally just ripening
150ml **rosehip syrup**
2 **lemons**, juiced
600ml **water**
80g **sugar**

Firstly make the plum puree, which will be added to the poaching liquor: cut the plums in half, remove the stones, then cut into quarters. Place the plum pieces in a small pan together with 50ml water and one dessert spoon caster sugar. Gently bring to the boil, and simmer for five minutes until the plums are soft. Press the plum pulp through a sieve to collect a smooth puree.

Place the puree into a pan together with all the remaining ingredients except the pears. Peel the pears and add to the poaching liquor. Cover the pears with the greaseproof paper to ensure they do not discolour during cooking. Gently bring the pears to the boil, simmer until just cooked through, remove from the heat and allow the pears to cool completely in the pan.

TO MAKE THE TURKISH DELIGHT

This recipe produces a very fruity Turkish delight with a deep red colour which is bursting with nuts. However, it has a less chewy texture than normal Turkish delight as this recipe does not use animal gelatine.

continued...

The recipe is quick to make, but may take an hour or so to set. The Turkish delight is best simply sliced into 2cm square cubes to serve with the poached pears, and is great as a confectionery rolled in icing sugar and cornflour.

This recipe makes about 750g and keeps in the fridge for two weeks.

200g **raspberry puree** (or 200g fresh/frozen raspberries, juice of half a **lemon**, plus 40ml **water**)
80g **flaked almonds**
50g shelled **pistachios**
200ml **water**
200g **caster sugar**

2 dessert spoons **rose water**
juice half **lemon**
2.5 teaspoons fine **agar agar powder**
25g **icing sugar** (optional, to serve as a confectionery)
25g **cornflour** (optional, to serve as a confectionery)

If you need to make the raspberry puree bring the raspberries, lemon juice and water to the boil, blend, then pass through a fine sieve.

Toast the almonds lightly until golden, either under a grill or in a preheated oven at 170°C for three to four minutes. Roughly chop the pistachios. Set both aside.

Add the raspberry puree, water, sugar and one dessert spoon of rose water to a pan and slowly bring to the boil to dissolve the sugar. Carefully whisk in the agar agar, simmer and whisk for four minutes to ensure it all dissolves and is completely integrated. It is best to test that the Turkish delight has set at this stage: take one spoonful and put on a cold plate, place in the fridge for five minutes. If it has not set, whisk in a further teaspoon of agar agar, simmer and stir carefully for a further two minutes. Remove from the heat and allow to cool for 10 minutes.

Mix in the remaining rose water, the toasted almonds and pistachio pieces.

The Turkish delight is now ready to set: line the tray with cling film. Pour in the Turkish delight and allow to set at room temperature for at least 30 minutes, then place in the fridge to fully set.

To serve: sieve the icing sugar and cornflour together and sprinkle evenly over a piece of greaseproof paper. Turn out the Turkish delight from the cling film onto the prepared paper. Using a sharp knife cut into 2cm square pieces. Toss well in the sugar mixture, then pack in an airtight container lined with waxed paper. Mix more icing sugar and cornflour together in equal quantities, then sprinkle over the sweets to stop them sticking together before covering the container.

Store in a cool, dry place for two weeks.

TUNISIAN ORANGE & PISTACHIO CAKE

with honey and saffron yoghurt

This simple-to-make, luxury cake has a coarse texture and deep, nutty orange flavour. It is delicious eaten as a plain cake, or can be served warm with drizzled honey and saffron yoghurt. Due to the volume of pistachios it is a little expensive to make, but can also be made by substituting 150g of ground almonds for 150g of pistachios.

SERVES 10

EQUIPMENT NEEDED: 20cm spring form cake tin; a food processor to grind the pistachios, plus ideally a mixer. Alternatively, the cake mix can be made by hand in a large bowl.

---

4 medium **eggs**

250g **caster sugar**

125g **butter**, melted

115g **extra virgin olive oil**

2 medium **oranges**, finely zested

250g **ground pistachios** (I did this in a blender)

70g fine **maize flour**

125g **plain flour**

1.5 heaped teaspoons **baking powder**

Juice two **oranges**, 50g **caster sugar** and a good pinch **cinnamon powder** for the syrup to seep the cake

50ml **clear honey**

200g **thick yoghurt**

half a **lime**, juiced

pinch of **saffron**

Preheat the oven to 150°C.

Grease and line a 20cm spring form cake tin with baking parchment. Beat together the eggs and caster sugar until thick and creamy. Slowly beat in the melted butter and the olive oil, a little at a time. Don't worry if the mixture splits as the dry ingredients will bring the mix back. Add the orange zest.

Mix together the ground pistachios, fine maize flour, plain flour and baking powder, and slowly fold into the wet ingredients. Transfer the mix to the prepared cake tin and bake for 50-60 minutes at 150°C. The cake should have doubled in size and be firm to the touch.

Cool for 30 minutes before seeping with the syrup.

For the orange drizzle place the orange juice, cinnamon and 50g caster sugar in a small pan. Bring to the boil slowly to ensure the sugar dissolves and reduce the liquid by one third, or until just thickening to a syrup.

continued...

Use a fine skewer to make 100 or so fine holes evenly throughout the surface of the cake. Slowly and evenly spoon on the syrup so the cake absorbs it all.

To make the saffron honey: mix the saffron with the lime juice in a bowl and leave for ten minutes for the saffron to diffuse. Mix in the thick yoghurt.

Serve the sliced cake either cold or warmed with drizzled honey and a good dollop of the saffron honey.

STRAWBERRY, ELDERFLOWER & LEMONGRASS PUNCH

This simple, fresh punch-style dessert has all the floral sweet flavours of early summer and is a real hit with adults and children alike. Substitute meadowsweet flowers for elderflowers in July, or add a little rum to make a light punch. This is best made 3-4 hours before serving.

SERVES 6   **EQUIPMENT NEEDED:** an attractive bowl to serve

500ml **water**

75g **caster sugar**

2 blades **lemongrass**, cut in half lengthways and then cut into 2cm strips

6 **elderflower heads**, carefully washed and shaken dry

600g **strawberries**, washed, stalks removed and cut in halves

Bring the water and sugar to the boil, stir to dissolve the sugar, add the lemongrass and allow to cool for 45 minutes until almost at room temperature.

Transfer the liquor to the serving bowl, add the lemon juice, strawberries and the elderflowers. Cover and place in the fridge to marinate for 3-4 hours before serving.

CHOCOLATE, ALMOND & PLUM PUDDING

with orange butterscotch sauce, and dairy-free coconut ice cream

This rich, super chocolatey bake is one of our most popular desserts at Tierra. The pudding is relatively simple to make, is vegan and can also be served as a brownie. This bake is so full of chocolate that we tend to make it a day in advance, which helps to slice and portion it neatly.

SERVES 12

EQUIPMENT NEEDED: baking tray/dish, size equivalent to 25cm x 25cm, with at least a 2.5cm depth; baking paper to line the baking tray/dish. A mixer is handy and quick, but the pudding can just as effectively be made by hand in a large bowl. If you want to include the ice cream; an ice cream churner

125g **flaked almonds**
400g **chocolate** with a 70% cocoa content, cut into 3mm pieces
225g **dairy-free margarine**
225g **caster sugar**
50ml **soya cream**
1 strong single **espresso** / 1 dessert spoon **coffee essence**

80g **plain flour**
1 heaped teaspoon **baking powder**
5 **dark plums**, stoned and cut into small pieces; roughly half a centimetre
Butterscotch sauce, *see recipe, page 21*
Dairy-free coconut ice cream, *see recipe, page 21*

Preheat the oven to 160°C.

Bake the almonds in the preheated oven for 6 to 8 minutes or until a light golden colour, set aside to cool.

Line the baking tray/dish with baking paper.

Melt half the chocolate and the margarine in a bain marie: mix 200g of the chocolate with the margarine in a sturdy bowl. Half fill a pan with water, place the bowl on top of the pan and put on a medium heat (by using this method the chocolate will not get too hot and split). Bring the pan gently to the boil, stir the chocolate and margarine until it has all melted, then remove the bowl from the hot water/heat.

In a mixer (or by hand) mix together the caster sugar and soya cream, then add the coffee. Next beat in the melted chocolate and margarine. Mix together the plain flour and baking powder and fold into the chocolate mix. Next mix in the plum pieces, then the toasted almonds. Finally, mix in the remaining 200g chocolate pieces. Transfer the mix evenly into the prepared baking tray, using a palette knife to ensure the mix is equally and smoothly dispersed.

continued...

Bake at 160°C for 35 minutes, or until a skewer cleanly exits the centre of the bake. NB: this pudding should be a little 'ganache' in the centre.

Remove from the oven, and either serve at once or allow to cool for 90 minutes, then refrigerate overnight; this way the pudding/brownie can be portioned into 12 neat portions with a sharp knife.

Serve with hot butterscotch sauce and a scoop of homemade dairy-free ice cream.

Come and see us at Tierra Kitchen
1A Coombe Street, Lyme Regis DT7 3PY

You can call us to make a reservation on
01297 445189 or book online at **www.tierrakitchen.co.uk**

Twitter **@TierraKitchen**
Facebook **TierraKitchenLymeRegis**

Author Mark Evans
Publisher Tierra Kitchen
Design danielhayman.com
Photography Terry Rook, Glance Image
Editing Sasa Jankovic